Growing Up for girls

EVERYTHING YOU NEED TO KNOW

Published in the UK by Scholastic, 2022
Euston House, 24 Eversholt Street, London, NW1 1DB
Scholastic Ireland, 89E Lagan Road, Dublin Industrial Estate, Glasnevin, Dublin, D11 HP5F

SCHOLASTIC and associated logos are trademarks and/or registered trademarks of Scholastic Inc.

Text © Dr Emily MacDonagh, 2022
Illustrations by Josefina Preumayr © Scholastic, 2022
Cover illustration by Josefina Preumayr
Author photograph © Holly Clark, 2021

Produced with the help of:
Emily Hibbs
Consultant Paediatrician: Dr Rebecca Mann
School Nurse: Charlene Hayes

Dr Emily MacDonagh is represented by The CAN Group **CAN**

ISBN 978 0702 3 1096 6

A CIP catalogue record for this book is available from the British Library.

Pap   ources.

This book is dedicated to all families who are trying to
navigate the journey through puberty.

To my amazing husband Pete, thank you for always supporting me.
Also, to our amazing collection of children: Junior, Princess, Millie and
Theo, who all keep me on my toes!

To my mum and dad who taught me pretty much everything you will read
here. Mum – I can't thank you enough for being my medical expert for this
book, although I think it was actually your parental expertise that helped
the most! Dad – your words of wisdom are invaluable to me.

Finally, to my little brothers (who are not so little any more)
Tom, Sam, Will and Joe.

I love you all xx

Growing Up for girls

EVERYTHING YOU NEED TO KNOW

DR EMILY MACDONAGH

ILLUSTRATED BY JOSEFINA PREUMAYR

SCHOLASTIC

Contents

Introduction

A BUMPY ROAD

Growing up is like travelling down a long, bumpy road. At the start, it seems like the road goes winding on for ever! There are twists and turns, and ups and downs. Sometimes it's a fun adventure, and sometimes it feels like the hardest journey in the world. All of us travel down this road, but we go at our own pace, in our own time. In this book, I'm going to help guide you down the road to growing up, pointing out the bumps, twists and turns along the way. By the time you've finished reading, you should know what to expect, and hopefully feel excited about the journey!

I'm sure you've heard of puberty. It's a word adults bring up a **LOT**, without always explaining what it's all about. Really, puberty just means growing up. It means all the changes our bodies go through to transform from a child into a teenager into an adult. The idea of puberty can sometimes seem a bit scary, but in this book I'll talk you through the changes – big and small – that are coming. Getting to grips with what your body might do before it starts doing it will mean there's no reason to feel worried or confused when things begin to happen.

NICE TO MEET YOU!

I'm **DR EMILY**, and I work for the National Health Service (NHS). I went to university for five years to study medicine, where I learned all about the changes children and young people go through during puberty. Then I started working as a doctor, which I have done for the last six years. I have worked in all sorts of places, and have loved meeting so many different people. Being a doctor can be tough, but it is also an amazing job because you can help people at difficult times in their lives.

I have four **(YES FOUR!)** younger brothers, who I watched grow up, and I have also seen my two stepchildren growing from infancy to Instagram! I am now bringing up my own children and I have really sussed out the easy bits, the hard bits and the questions everyone wants to ask about puberty but are too embarrassed to… I've had lots of practice in explaining how growing up works over the years and now I've put all that knowledge in a book so that YOU can find out all about it too. The most important thing I want you to know is that no question is silly or embarrassing. If you want to know the answer to something, chances are someone else will too. The more we speak out and ask those tricky questions, the easier it will become for everyone to get the information they need!

Over the following few chapters, I'll take you through the journey of puberty, explaining the things that will happen to your body and why. This book is mostly about girls' bodies, but we'll have a quick chat about what's happening to the boys, too. Before we get into it, let's start with this book's most important message:

YOU ARE TOTALLY UNIQUE!
Everyone goes through puberty in their own way, at their own time.
THERE REALLY IS NO RIGHT OR WRONG WAY TO GROW UP.

MIND MAYHEM

During puberty, as well as physical changes, your mind will go through changes, too. Sometimes the changes in the way you think and feel can seem even scarier than the changes happening in your body. You might feel really moody sometimes, or your emotions might go wild. This is all a normal part of growing up, and things will soon settle down, I promise! Remember, every adult you know has already gone through puberty. Everyone from your granny, to your head teacher to your favourite popstar, YouTuber or TikToker. If they can do it, so can you. **YOU ARE NOT ALONE**.

There are lots of fantastic things about growing up – you can become more independent, get your dream job, and earn your own money. You can travel around the world, explore new places and meet new friends. You can start making decisions about what you want to do and who you want to be, so that you can make the most of your life. But to get from where you are now to where you'll end up, you'll have to travel down that long, bumpy road we were talking about earlier. By reading this book and finding out all about puberty, you might not make the road any smoother, but at least you'll know what bumps are coming!

Ready to get started?

What's the Point of Puberty?

You might be wondering why we all have to go through puberty in the first place. **WHY DO OUR BODIES NEED TO CHANGE? THEY WORK PERFECTLY WELL AS THEY ARE, DON'T THEY?** The changes that happen during puberty get your **BODY AND BRAIN** ready **TO BE AN ADULT** so you can do things like have a baby if you want to. Not everyone wants to have, or can have, children and that's fine! But it's still important for your body and brain to develop during puberty. Sometimes, people focus on the changes they can see, but the changes you feel inside are just as important. You'll discover new things about yourself and get to know your feelings. You might start becoming interested in different activities and develop close friendships with new people.

There are lots of tricky terms to keep track of when we talk about puberty and growing up. You'll find a list of the most important ones in the glossary at the back of the book.

ALL CHANGE!

Here are a few of the changes girls go through during puberty. We'll look at all of these in much more detail later in the book.

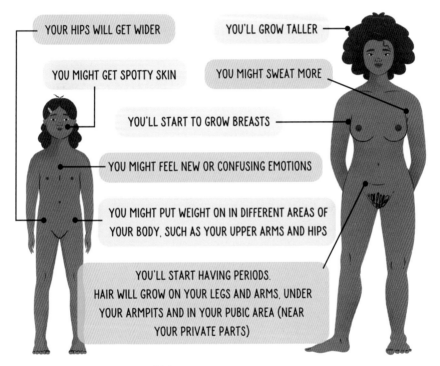

YOUR HIPS WILL GET WIDER

YOU'LL GROW TALLER

YOU MIGHT GET SPOTTY SKIN

YOU MIGHT SWEAT MORE

YOU'LL START TO GROW BREASTS

YOU MIGHT FEEL NEW OR CONFUSING EMOTIONS

YOU MIGHT PUT WEIGHT ON IN DIFFERENT AREAS OF YOUR BODY, SUCH AS YOUR UPPER ARMS AND HIPS

YOU'LL START HAVING PERIODS. HAIR WILL GROW ON YOUR LEGS AND ARMS, UNDER YOUR ARMPITS AND IN YOUR PUBIC AREA (NEAR YOUR PRIVATE PARTS)

It sounds like a lot of **BIG** changes when you see them all together like that, doesn't it? Don't worry, you're not going to wake up one day looking and feeling completely different. These changes will happen over months or even years, and you'll have plenty of time to get used to them.

Part One:

CHANGES IN YOUR BODY

Getting Kick-started

When it comes to puberty, your brain runs the show. A special part of your brain, called the pituitary gland, has a very important role to play. You can think of it like the conductor of an orchestra, telling each of your body parts what they need to do and when. First, it tells your body to grow and change in different ways. Then, it tells your emotions and thinking to mature, too, so that you're ready to deal with life as an adult. The only trouble is, your body develops before your mind, so you might not always feel ready for the changes!

Your brain organizes things in your body so you gradually move from being a child to being a teenager (also called 'ADOLESCENCE') to being an adult. These changes happen at different times for different people. There's no right age for them to begin but puberty usually begins sometime between the ages of eight and fourteen. When the brain decides it's time, it sends out some messages to get things going. It does this through chemicals called hormones, which act like messengers travelling around your body. Here's how it happens:

STEP ONE: your brain sends a message to your ovaries to start making a hormone called oestrogen.

STEP TWO: the oestrogen slips into your bloodstream and arrives at your breast area. Here, it triggers your breasts to start growing.

STEP THREE: a gland in your tummy starts producing a whole new set of hormones, called androgens. Androgens are even more important for boys, but they have some jobs to do in girls, too…

STEP FOUR: the androgens make hair grow under your armpits and around your genitals.

STEP FIVE: meanwhile, the oestrogen is still busy making further changes. As well as making your boobs bigger, it also makes your genitals bigger, and your uterus increases in size so that your body is ready to have a baby some day, if you want to. Girls' genitals are mostly on the inside of their bodies. This is what they look like:

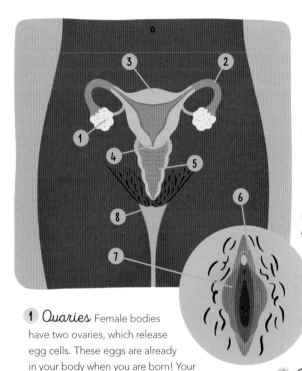

female bodies where babies grow during pregnancy. It stretches to get bigger as a baby inside it grows.

4 *Cervix* The opening at the bottom of the uterus, which connects it to the vagina.

5 *Vagina* A stretchy tube which connects your uterus to the outside of your body. During your period, blood travels out of your body through your vagina. It is also where babies are born from.

6 *Clitoris* A small, round bump at the top of your labia, which is very sensitive.

7 *Labia* Folds of skin that protect your vagina, which get bigger during puberty.

8 *Urethra* The tube through which urine leaves the body.

1 *Ovaries* Female bodies have two ovaries, which release egg cells. These eggs are already in your body when you are born! Your body doesn't make new ones, so you have a limited amount. When you start your periods, your body releases an egg from your ovary around once a month.

2 *Fallopian tubes* Tubes connecting your ovaries to your uterus, which your eggs travel down.

3 *Uterus (womb)* The organ in

As well as your vagina, you have two other openings near your genital area. The urethra is where your urine (wee) comes out, and the anus is where your faeces (poo) comes out. These don't change during puberty, though.

Just in case you were wondering, here's what boys' genitals look like:

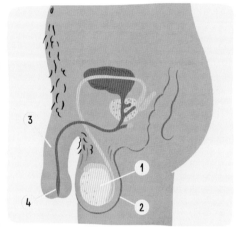

1 *Testicles* Two balls which make sperm. They also make hormones (especially testosterone) which trigger changes in boys' bodies during puberty.

2 *Scrotum* A bag of skin which holds a boy's testicles.

3 *Penis* An organ which leads from the inside of a boys' body to the outside. The urethra runs through the penis, so boys wee out of the opening at the end of their penis, and it can also release sperm. Sperm are special cells which, if they meet with an egg in a female body, can grow into a baby.

4 *Urethra* The tube through which urine leaves the body.

IN YOUR OWN TIME

Everyone goes into puberty at different times. There's no need to panic if you are the smallest person in the class and everyone else seems to be growing boobs and starting their periods. It might feel like you're tiny, and that you'll be 'left behind' for ever. But remember the story of the hare and the tortoise? The speedy hare challenged the slow tortoise to a race, thinking it would be an easy win. The hare sprinted off so fast he shot **MILES** ahead of the plodding tortoise. But then the hare stopped for a quick break, and fell asleep under a tree. The tortoise shuffled on, overtook the hare and won the race!

Being one of the last to go through puberty is a bit like that. You might feel left behind when everyone else is having their growth spurts, but once they've stopped growing you'll catch them up, and may even overtake them. Of course, puberty isn't a race, and it's not something you can 'win'. But it's important not to worry if you're more of a tortoise than a hare – just remember you'll get there in the end!

MAKING A BABY

In this book I say that the physical purpose of puberty is to get your body ready to have a baby when you are a fully grown adult. The diagrams so far have shown you the parts of your body that are important during puberty but it is also worth talking about how you actually get pregnant because it can seem a bit confusing at first.

To make a baby you need a male sperm and a female egg. On page 15 there is a diagram of a boy's genitals where we talk about sperm, the special cells that if they meet an egg in a female body, can grow into a baby. *The million dollar question is how does the sperm get to the egg?*

The sperm are created in the testicles, down in the boys' scrotum, and the female's egg is made inside the tummy in the ovary.

When a woman and her partner feel they are ready to have a baby they have sex – the proper name for this is *'sexual intercourse'*. When grown-ups know each other well and are in love, sex is a normal part of a caring adult relationship. During sex, the man's sperm is released into the vagina and if the sperm meets the egg, that's when the egg can be fertilized and the woman can become pregnant. This is the earliest part of growing a baby.

CLEVER CHEMICALS

There are lots of different hormones whizzing around your body during puberty, all doing different jobs. For girls, two of the most important hormones are oestrogen and progesterone. Progesterone's main job is to make changes in your uterus (the part of your body where a baby grows). Oestrogen causes many different changes in your body, including…

Making breast tissue grow.

Making you grow taller. Some hormones will make you grow taller, but when you have more oestrogen in your body it will actually slow your growth down. This explains why women are generally shorter than men.

Encouraging your body to store fat in different areas, such as your hips, thighs and breasts. This means that women often have more fat in their bodies than men, which is completely normal and healthy.

WHAT HAPPENS WHEN?

For most girls, puberty follows a fixed order once it has got started. That looks something like this:

1 You might notice small, hard lumps called *breast buds* behind your nipples. That's your breasts beginning to grow.

2 You might start to make a bit more sweat under your armpits, and generally get a bit more *'smelly'* when you're doing sport or feeling hot.

3 *Hair* will start growing in your armpits and around your private parts.

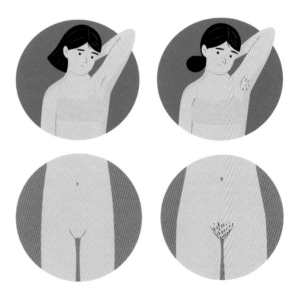

4 The outside bits of your genitals (*the labia*) will get a bit bigger and more noticeable.

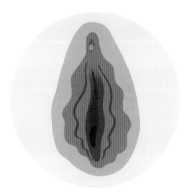

5 Gradually, you'll get more armpit hair and more hair around your private parts. Your boobs will continue growing. (Eventually they will reach a *'final size'* and stop growing, but that might take several years.)

6 You'll start your **periods**. That's a whole new set of changes that we'll talk about later, or you can flick ahead to page 33 now!

It is common to be curious about the changes that are happening to your body. Everyone has a look at themselves in the mirror – it's how you get to know your body. It is perfectly normal to want to know about the changes that are happening to your body, so don't be embarrassed to feel about and check on things or even ask a parent if you're worried that something isn't normal.

Developing Breasts

One of the first signs of puberty is your breasts beginning to grow. The first thing you might notice is a small lump the size of a pea or button under your nipple, called a breast bud. The breast buds might feel a bit painful in the shower, or when your roll over in bed or play sport. In fact, when your breasts start to develop, they can feel really tender! This is because your body is growing some completely new tissue. As the skin and breast tissue grows, it stretches and is really delicate. The hormones in your body can also make your breasts feel a bit painful, but this is a normal part of breast development and is nothing to worry about. When your periods start, you might notice your breasts are painful at certain times before or during your period, too. This is also because of the hormones in your body, and is completely normal.

As your boobs begin growing, they'll usually start off quite pointy. The darker skin around your nipple (the areola) can be raised. In time, your boobs will become a more rounded shape. It can several years for them to grow to their final size.

ASK DOCTOR EMILY

Q: One of my boobs is bigger than the other. Am I weird?

A: Definitely not! It's really common to have one boob bigger than the other, just like how lots of people have one foot slightly bigger than the other. Your boobs also might not grow at the same time, or at the same speed. You might think there's a really noticeable difference between their sizes, only for them to even out a few months later.

Even if the difference in your boob size seems like the most obvious thing in the world to you, I promise you no one else will have a clue. If you're feeling really worried or self-conscious, you could talk to an adult you trust about it, and consider putting a little bit of padding on the smaller side, just for your own peace of mind.

Boobs come in all shapes and sizes, so whatever yours end up looking like, they are totally normal!

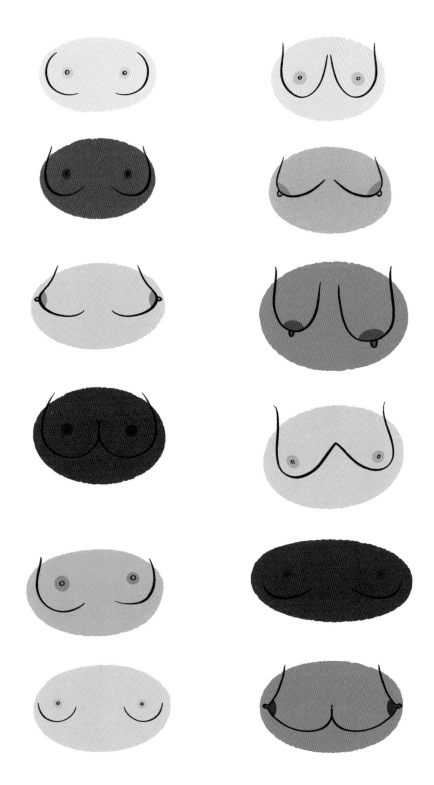

CHOOSING A BRA

When your boobs get bigger and heavier, you might want to consider wearing a bra. You 100% don't have to wear a bra if you don't want to, but you might find that your boobs are a bit uncomfortable when you're doing sport or running around, particularly if they are big. Bras can give your boobs support and make things comfier for you in your day-to-day life.

If you do want to start wearing a bra, some shops offer a *bra-fitting service*, or there are lots of *online guides* for how to measure your own chest before you go bra shopping. Here are some tips for finding the best bra:

A GOOD BRA SHOULD...

- fit snugly around your chest
- have cups that fit comfortably around your boobs

A GOOD BRA SHOULD NOT...

- have straps that dig in to your shoulders
- pinch or scratch your skin
- leave pink marks on your back (that means it's too tight)

Growth Spurts

During puberty and your teenage years, you'll grow
very fast. When you were little, you grew about two to five
centimetres a year. Amazingly, during puberty, this increases
to a whopping ten centimetres a year! So, you grow nearly
four times faster during puberty than at any other
time in your life.

So, how does all the growing stuff happen? Once again, the *pituitary gland* – the conductor of the orchestra in your brain – is in charge of telling all the other parts of your body what to do. The pituitary gland produces special hormones known as growth hormones. Your brain mainly produces growth hormones while you're sound asleep at night. This is actually one of the reasons why you need more sleep as a teenager – more time snoozing means more time for your brain to get to work making those growth hormones!

These special hormones mostly affect the growth of your bones. As your bones get longer, they gradually stretch your muscles and ligaments. This stretching is why you might find you get *'growing pains'* – aches and pains in your arms and legs. As your muscles and ligaments get tugged and tightened, it can be uncomfortable, especially at night. This will get better with time, but if you're feeling a bit sore or achy, try sleeping with a hot water bottle.

TALL OR SHORT?

The thing about your height is you can't really change it, so it's best to find a way to be happy as you are, whether you're the shortest girl in your class, or the tallest. People of all different heights achieve amazing things, and sometimes their height can play a factor in that. If you're small, you might be really good at horse riding or gymnastics. If you're tall, you could be great at long jump or rowing. However, that doesn't mean you can't be good at the things you enjoy whatever height or body shape you are.

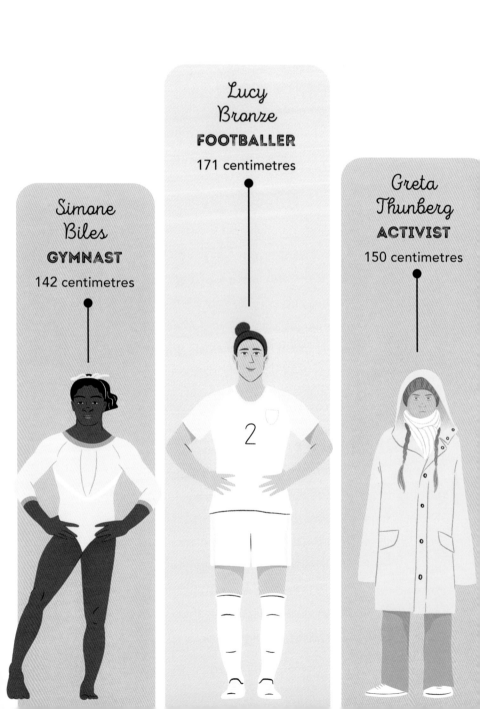

Simone
Biles
GYMNAST

142 centimetres

Lucy
Bronze
FOOTBALLER

171 centimetres

Greta
Thunberg
ACTIVIST

150 centimetres

2

Zendaya
ACTRESS AND SINGER
177 centimetres

Maria Sharapova
RETIRED TENNIS PLAYER
188 centimetres

Malala Yousafzai
ACTIVIST
161 centimetres

Changing Shape

As well as growing taller, your body will also change shape during puberty. Most girls put on a bit of weight as their body stores fat in different places. Along with your boobs getting bigger, your hips will widen. Your wider hips might make your waist look smaller, and make the top of your thighs a bit wider. All bodies are good bodies, so try not to compare your shape to your friends' or to girls you see on social media.

Sometimes, it's really easy to be critical about yourself. We often break ourselves down into little bits, focusing on the things we don't like about our bodies. It's strange, because we don't see other people that way! We don't look at our friends and see a collection of body parts; we see them for the wonderful people they are.

So, let's try and see ourselves that way, too – as whole people.

As your body changes, try to focus on the things that make you feel contented and confident as a whole person, and don't worry about the shapes and sizes of different bits of your body.

Down Below

Remember oestrogen, that important hormone that makes your boobs grow? Well, it makes some things grow bigger in your genital area, too. This is where the organs involved in making babies are and that's exactly why they change – to get your body ready to have a baby some day if you want to.

Most of this development goes on inside your body, but you'll see a few signs on the outside too. Your *clitoris* and *labia* will get bigger and change shape. Because we don't see each other's bits and bobs, it's easy to worry that yours look strange. I'm telling you now, they definitely don't! **Everyone's private parts look different**, and there's a huge range of shapes and sizes! And guess what? **THEY'RE ALL NORMAL...**

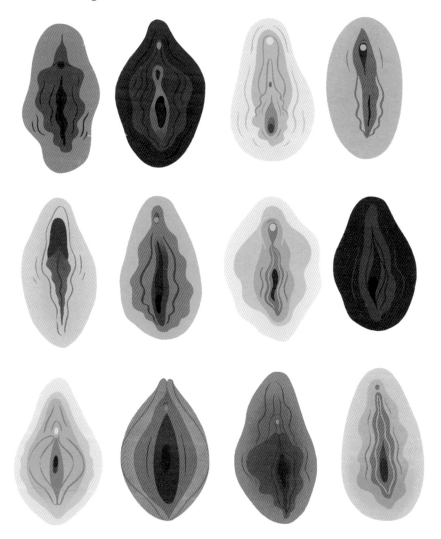

Oestrogen also makes the tissue in your genitals softer, and they start making a small amount of whiteish liquid to keep the delicate skin moisturized. This liquid might start appearing in your pants at the earliest stage of puberty, often at about the same time your boobs start growing. This liquid is called discharge, which is a bit of an icky name, but it's nothing to be worried or ashamed about. All women have it, and it helps to keep their private parts clean and healthy.

Some people stick on thin pads (liners) into their pants if the discharge bothers them, but most girls and women don't. Showering or having a bath and changing your pants each day is all you need to do to keep things clean down there.

Starting Your Period

Starting your periods and learning how to deal with them so they don't bother you can sometimes be the trickiest part of growing up for girls. If you're feeling a bit panicky about the idea of periods, I hope that by the end of this section, you feel more clued-up so that when yours does start, it doesn't faze you. Some people might call your period other names, like '*menstruation*' or '*time of the month*'.

As I've mentioned, puberty is your body getting ready so you could have a baby in the future, if you wanted to. To do this, your body has to start releasing an egg each month. If the egg meets a sperm, it becomes '*fertilized*' and has a chance of growing into a baby in the future. The egg travels from the ovary to your uterus **(see diagram 1 below)**, which has developed a lining in which the fertilized egg can plant itself and then possibly grow into a baby over the nine months of a pregnancy. If the egg isn't fertilized, the egg and the lining of the uterus pass out of your body, through your vagina **(see diagram 2)**. This means that each month, you'll have a bit of bleeding for a few days as the lining of the uterus is passed.

Everyone loses a different amount of blood each month: this is how '*heavy*' your period is. The funny thing is, it can feel like you lose a lot of blood, but actually most people only lose a tiny amount each time! The average person will lose about six to eight teaspoons of blood with each period, with some losing a little more and some a little less.

1

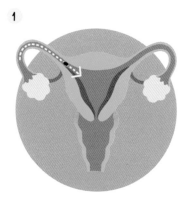

2

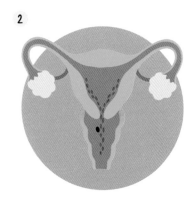

ASK DOCTOR EMILY

Q: *How do I know when my period is going to start for the first time?*

A: It's very hard to predict the exact day or week that your period is going to start, and it often takes people by surprise. It's helpful to look for your body's signs that your first period might be on its way. This means you can get ready by keeping a few period products in your school bag, so you're prepared and ready to go, wherever and whenever you come on your period.

Signs to look out for are:

o   whiteish discharge in your underwear

o   your breasts starting to grow

o   hair growing in your armpits or pubic area.

Once you notice these signs, your periods are likely to start within a year or so. Do remember though that everyone is different, and everyone will see slightly different changes to their body before their periods start.

WHAT TO EXPECT

When you first start your period, you'll see some blood in your pants or when you wipe yourself after going to the loo.

The blood isn't coming from a cut or injury, so it doesn't hurt. However, because the muscles of your uterus squeeze a bit to help the egg and lining pass through, you might get a gripey pain in your tummy. The blood itself is not a sign of damage – it's just your body showing it's working properly.

Having periods is not a secret or bad thing, and people often let their friends or parents know when it is their period. You don't need to feel embarrassed or ashamed when you are having your period. You are not dirty or gross. Unless you tell them, most people will have absolutely no idea it's your time of the month anyway. Periods can feel personal though, so it's good to be able to manage that bit of blood independently, that way you can do what you want without worrying about being uncomfortable, and go where you want while feeling confident!

SANITARY PRODUCTS

During your period, you'll need to use or wear something to stop any blood leaking out or getting on your pants or clothes. There are several different period products, sometimes called *sanitary products*, designed to stop that bit of blood from causing any bother.

Sanitary towels (pads) can be different shapes and thicknesses. You stick them in your pants and change them every few hours. You might need a larger, thicker pad at the start of

your period and at night, and then a
smaller, thinner one when there is less
blood, towards the end of your period.

Tampons look a bit like a stick of cotton wool with a short string
at the end. They fit inside your vagina, where they
absorb the blood. Tampons take a bit of time to
get used to, but once you have got the hang of
inserting them, they're easy to manage. They are
also really useful, as you can go swimming when
wearing a tampon, but you can't when wearing
a sanitary towel.

The key to making a tampon feel comfortable is putting it far
enough inside your vagina – if it is half in, half out it will be
uncomfortable, but when it is in the right place you won't feel
it at all. Some tampons have *'applicators'* which make it easier
to push them into your vagina. A tampon without an applicator
needs to be gently pushed in with your finger, which can be a
bit fiddly to begin with. In the same way you wouldn't roughly
poke something into your nose or your ear, you'll want to be
gentle with yourself when you're putting a tampon in.

Most girls just starting their periods use towels and tampons,
and that's what we focus on for this book. But there are other
period products available too, including *eco-friendly period
pants, period cups* and *reusable pads*.

These have the added benefit of being kind to the environment:

Period pants have extra layers to absorb
blood. You rinse them out with cold
water and pop them in the wash after
each use.

Reusable pads can be rinsed, washed and
worn again.

Period cups are small funnel-shaped cups which you
put in your vagina, a bit like a tampon. They can be
emptied, washed and used again.

If you're feeling curious, why not ask an adult you trust if you
can buy a few different period products to have a look at? Take
them out of their packets and investigate how they work. If you
have a think about what product, or combination of products,
might be right for you when the time comes now, then that'll
be one less thing to worry about!

KEEPING FRESH, STAYING SAFE

You'll need to change your period product regularly to stop it
leaking or becoming uncomfortable. The heavier your period
(the more blood you have) the more often you'll need to
change. Periods can last anywhere from three to eight days;

they are often heaviest for the first two to three days, so you might need to change a pad or tampon every time you go to the toilet to begin with, perhaps four or five times a day. As the week goes on, your period will get lighter, so you might only need to change two or three times a day.

Changing your tampon is especially important. Swapping your tampon every four to six hours or so is best, and you shouldn't leave it in longer than eight hours. Leaving in a tampon for several days can cause a very rare but very serious infection called *toxic-shock syndrome*, so it really is important not to forget!

Choose the smallest-sized tampon possible for your flow. If you notice that your tampon isn't full when you go to change it, you could try a smaller size. If your period is really heavy, it's fine to wear both a tampon and a pad, just to be on the safe side and avoid any annoying leaks. However, you shouldn't have to do this regularly, so consider visiting your doctor if you're having really heavy periods every month.

WHAT SHOULD I DO WITH MY USED SANITARY TOWEL OR TAMPON?

There are special bins in most girls' toilets for tampons and sanitary towels. Just wrap your used pad in the wrapper of the fresh pad you've stuck in your pants, and then chuck it away.

If you can't see a special bin, don't panic. You can just wrap your pad or tampon up in a bit of toilet paper and put it in a normal bin – **no problem!** The only thing you shouldn't do is flush your used pad or tampon down the loo – it could block pipes, and even end up in rivers or oceans where it can harm the environment.

ASK DOCTOR EMILY

Q: *Will my periods hurt?*

A: It is common to feel a bit of pain in your lower tummy when you have your period. Sometimes the pain can begin a day or two before you start having blood. The reason for this is that the muscle inside your uterus is busy squeezing the lining out. You also might not feel any pain, but your tummy might feel a bit uncomfortable or bloated.

For most people, the pain isn't too bad and can be managed by having a rest or hugging a hot-water bottle. Some people choose to take painkillers like ibuprofen or paracetamol, but you should chat to an adult first before taking any tablets or medicine.

For a few people, periods can be really painful and have

a big impact on their lives. If your period pain is stopping you from doing things you enjoy or making you feel down then it's a good idea to chat to an adult about arranging to see your doctor. Your doctor can let you know some different options to help make things better for you.

NO PERIOD PANIC!

Still feeling nervous? Don't be! Here are my top tips for handling your time of the month, easy-peasy.

Always carry a period product so you don't get caught off guard. You can tuck it in a pocket or bag so that no matter when or where your period starts, you can pop to the loo and sort things out.

While you're still getting used to your periods, there's no harm in going to the toilet a bit more regularly than you need to. This way, you can check for leaks and change your period product often. Try going every break or lunchtime at school, and every couple of hours at home.

Carry a spare pair of pants in your bag, just in case!

HEAVY PERIODS

Look out for signs that your period is really heavy, for example if you are having to change your period products more than every two hours. Another clue is if you are often bleeding right through to your clothing or bedding. If this is happening to you, it is something you should mention to an adult you trust, such as a parent or school nurse. You can then decide whether to chat to a doctor about things you could do to help make your periods more manageable. Lots of doctors are women, and you can always ask to speak to a female doctor if that would make you feel more comfortable when you're chatting about period stuff.

PERIODS AND MOODS

Some girls find that they can feel a bit grumpy or down in the dumps in the run up to their periods. This is sometimes called *'being pre-menstrual'* or *'pre-menstrual syndrome'*. It's a sign of the changing hormones that your body is producing. It doesn't usually affect girls when they are just starting their periods and, so long as you know about it and understand why you are feeling a bit out of sorts, it's not something to be worried about. If bad moods from pre-menstrual syndrome are causing you problems though, it might be worth talking to your doctor about how you're feeling.

PERIOD PLANNING

When you first start your periods, you might find that they aren't very regular. Perhaps you bleed for a few days one month, then nothing happens for several months, then you have some blood again. **Eventually, this will settle into a pattern.** It's good to make a note of when you start each period, so you can make a good guess at when the next one might come. This way, you can have everything you need ready for when it arrives. Generally speaking, you start your period every twenty-eight days, but anywhere between twenty-one and thirty-five days is normal.

ASK DOCTOR EMILY

Q: *What if I don't start puberty between eight and fourteen? Is there something wrong with me?*

A: If you notice changes in your body happening before you are eight, then you don't need to feel worried. Speak to a parent or an adult you trust, and they may suggest going to see your doctor. Very often it is nothing to worry about; for example, going through puberty early may just run in your family! Sometimes your doctor might want to check you for certain things that can cause puberty to start early.

If you are over fourteen and haven't started puberty, this may also just be something that runs in your family and often is nothing to worry about. Just like early puberty, it is a good idea to speak to an adult you trust if you are feeling anxious. They might suggest seeing your doctor to make sure everything is OK. It is very unusual for early or late puberty to be a sign of any important problem – you might just be a tortoise or a hare!

Hairy Bits

So, as we've seen already, there's a LOT going on in your body during puberty. The conductor of it all – your brain – is busy composing a symphony of changes. Then, it brings in yet another part: a hormone called *testosterone*. In boys' bodies, testosterone is kind of like the lead musician, but in girls' bodies, it has a less dramatic part to play.

An increase in the levels of *testosterone* in girls' bodies contributes to growth spurts. Along with androgens, testosterone also makes a different kind of hair grow in your armpits and pubic area. The hair is usually quite dark and thick. It'll be more noticeable than your other body hair but it doesn't grow very long. Like growing boobs, or getting discharge, having hair in your armpits and pubic areas is normal and everybody – **EVERYBODY** – has it.

Axillary (armpit) hair

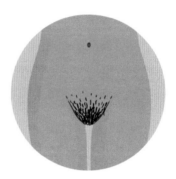
Pubic hair

YOUR BRILLIANT BODY HAIR

Your body goes through a real hair journey starting from the day you are born! Newborn babies are covered in a type of hair called '*lanugo hair*'. The job of this hair is to help protect the baby's skin from the fluid in their mum's tummy. After the baby is born, the lanugo hair starts to be replaced with a different type of hair, called '*vellus hair*'.

Vellus hair helps keep your body at the right temperature. It looks pale, short and fluffy, and covers most of your skin –

even your eyelids! During puberty, your hair changes again and becomes '*terminal*'. Sounds a bit scary, but all this means is that some of the hair on your body becomes thicker and darker, like the hair on your head (but shorter!). These terminal hairs grow under your armpits and around your genital area, but the more androgens you have, the more areas of your body might grow this type of hair. As boys have more androgens, they are generally hairier!

LOSE IT OR LEAVE IT?

As you get older, the amount of hair in your armpits and pubic area will gradually increase. What you do with it is totally up to you. Some girls choose to leave it just as it is. Some girls choose to remove their armpit hair by shaving, waxing or using hair-removal cream. Some girls also choose to remove parts of their pubic hair, so that it doesn't show when they go swimming, for example. Also, some girls choose to remove hair from their legs. You should do whatever makes you feel the most comfortable and confident. Whatever you decide, you should **NEVER EVER** worry about your body hair. It's normal, natural and all part of growing up.

Whether you choose to remove your body hair is a personal choice, and you shouldn't feel pressure to do so. If you do choose to get rid of it, spend some time looking into the different methods, and the pros and cons of each. Bear in mind that removing hair can cause rashes, ingrown hair (hairs that grow under your skin) and spots, so do it carefully and ask for advice from a trusted adult first. It's not a one-time thing, either! Like the hair on your head, body hair does grow back and will need to be shaved, waxed or removed with cream repeatedly, if you do decide you don't want it on your body.

ASK DOCTOR EMILY

Q: *I've got hair on my face! Should I get rid of it?*

A: Lots of girls develop fine facial hair, commonly on their upper lip. Before you even think about removing any facial hair, trying stepping back from the mirror to see if it's really as noticeable as you think. You might believe that it's super obvious, when in reality nobody else can see it. If you're still concerned about it, or would just feel happier with it gone, talk to an adult you trust about the different options for bleaching, thinning or removing it. Make sure you have your parent's permission before trying any products though and remember that the skin on your face can be especially sensitive. It's not a good idea to shave it, as the stubble that grows back will probably feel prickly and look darker as it hasn't been exposed to the sun. That means you'll end up having to shave it over and over again.

Very rarely, excessive facial hair can be a sign of a medical condition. If you are worried about your hair growth, it's a good idea to talk to your doctor.

Getting Sweaty

You've already discovered how amazing your body is, but the truth is, it is a bit fussy, too. It likes to be at the exact temperature of 37°C for everything to work properly. Luckily, your body has some tricks up its sleeve to keep itself at exactly this temperature. Sweat is one of the ways your body cools itself down when you start to get too warm, like when the weather is really sunny or when you are exercising. Your body's temperature can also rise due to hormonal changes, illness or stress, so your body will sweat more at these times too.

When you start to get a bit hot, your brain sends hormone messengers around your body to tell it to get *sweating*. Sweat glands, which live just below the skin, respond to these messages by mixing up water, salt and a few other bits. This sweat leaves your body through invisible holes in your skin called *pores*. When the sweat reaches the air, it turns into vapour and evaporates, like how a puddle disappears on a hot day. This process of evaporation is what cools your skin down.

You need to drink plenty of water when you're sweaty, to replace the water you're losing through sweat. If you've ever tasted your own sweat (like when it's streaming down your face during PE!) you'll have noticed it tastes salty. No matter how much sport you do, and how much you sweat, as long as you drink plenty of water and eat a healthy balanced diet your body will sort out your fluid and salt balance.

STINKY SWEAT?

I bet you've heard one of your classmates walk into the changing rooms and shout something like:

> **"Urgh, it STINKS of sweat in here!"**

The smell we associate with sweat can be pretty strong, and it's not always very pleasant!

The interesting thing is that sweat doesn't smell at all. It's actually bacteria on your skin breaking down your sweat that causes the '*body odour*' smell! Often, we don't notice our own body smelling and a parent or friend might decide to kindly point it out to us… Try not to take offence and remember it's a normal part of becoming an adult and pretty easy to sort out. Make sure you are washing with soap every day, and most people also use a deodorant or antiperspirant (*which literally means 'anti sweat'!*) to keep body odour at bay. A combination of the two is best.

There's no specific age you should begin using deodorant or antiperspirant but if you notice your underarms feeling sweaty or smelling whiffy, that's probably a good time to start. Deodorants add a nice smell and just cover up any stronger smells from your armpits whereas antiperspirants actually stop you from sweating, or dry up your sweat. These products come as *roll-ons, gels, sprays* and *creams* and you can buy them in any pharmacy or supermarket. Most people put on an antiperspirant every time they wash or shower, so possibly even a couple of times a day.

Keep in mind that some people don't need to use deodorant or antiperspirant at all. You've probably seen some silly deodorant adverts that try to convince you you'll clear a room of people if you don't buy their products… If you're lucky enough to be able to tackle your body odour just by taking regular baths or showers and wearing clean clothes, then don't feel the pressure to buy something you don't need.

ASK DOCTOR EMILY

Q: *Does having armpit hair make you sweat more?*

A: The amount that you sweat depends on lots of factors, and is individual to you. Having armpit hair doesn't make you produce more sweat. However, hair can hold moisture, so if you have hair under your armpits it can make you feel like you are more sweaty. This sweat can lead to body odour, as more sweat means more bacteria breaking it down.

This doesn't mean you need to remove the hair from your armpits though. As long as you are washing daily and using deodorant if you need to then having armpit hair shouldn't lead to having smelly armpits. Some women remove their armpit hair purely because they prefer the way it looks, but some choose to remove the hair to stop sweat becoming trapped in it.

Keeping Clean

The best way to keep clean is to have a bath or a shower every day using mild soap and warm water. This will help to clear away any bacteria, stopping it from making nasty smells!

If you've got sensitive skin or eczema, be especially careful with the kind of soaps and body washes you use. Check with a doctor or skin specialist about the kind of products that are right for you, and avoid scrubbing any sore areas of your skin. After you've had a bath or a shower, you should pat your skin lightly, so it still stays a bit damp. This will help your skin absorb any cream, gel or moisturizer you've been prescribed.

When it comes to your private parts, the inside of your vagina is perfectly capable of cleaning itself – I mentioned the whiteish discharge, this is simply your body's way of keeping things clean. You should gently wash the outside of your vagina with *plain, unperfumed soap* every day. Avoid using perfumed soaps as they can affect the delicate balance of bacteria and the pH level (the acid/alkaline level) in the vagina, and might even irritate it. During your period, it's a good idea to wash the area more than once a day.

HAIR CARE

The hormones that make your skin oily and create acne are the same ones that can have an effect on your hair. Each strand of hair has its own gland that produces oil, which keeps your hair shiny and waterproof. During puberty, the glands produce extra oils – this can make your hair look nice and shiny, but sometimes it gets a bit too shiny and ends up greasy.

How often you should wash your hair depends on how greasy it gets! Some people only need to wash their hair once a week, whereas others find their hair gets greasy after just a day or two. If that's you, there are some special shampoos made for oily hair. When you do wash it, use warm water and just a small blob of shampoo to make lots of bubbles. Don't rub or scrub too hard, as that might damage your hair or irritate your scalp. After rinsing, you can use a conditioner if you like, but pick one that's suitable for oily hair if you need to. If you want to use products to style your hair, remember some will add extra grease, which might mean you need to wash your hair more often. It's a good idea to keep your brushes and combs clean too, as otherwise they'll transfer grease and dirt back into your clean hair.

FEELING FRESH

It's important to wear clean clothes, socks and underwear each day. Natural materials, like cotton, wool and bamboo are better at absorbing sweat than synthetic (artificial) materials like polyester and Lycra. But whatever your clothes are made from, you can still keep them feeling fresh and smelling clean! You just need to make sure you wash them regularly and that your body is clean when you put them on, too.

You should also change the sheets on your bed for fresh ones every one to two weeks. The sweatier you are at night, the more regularly you should switch your sheets!

Skin and Spots

Every inch of your skin is covered in hundreds of
tiny glands which produce and release substances, like
sweat or oil. Sebaceous glands are a type of gland which
release oil, also known as *'sebum'*, into your skin to keep
it healthy. When you begin puberty, these glands respond
to the hormones rushing round your body and start working
overtime, making more oils. They are especially sensitive
to testosterone, and the more testosterone in your body,
the more oil they will produce.

Though these oils help keep your skin moisturized and stop it from drying out, they can also cause spots or acne. *Acne* is mainly caused by the hormone changes that are happening in your body. A build up of oil and bacteria on the surface of your skin can make it easier for spots to form. These things clog up your pores, along with your follicles (the places the tiny hairs on the surface of your skin grow from). When a clogged pore is on the surface of your skin, it can make a **whitehead**. Sometimes a clogged pore stays open, which is called a **blackhead**. The bacteria on your skin can make spots bigger, more inflamed and sorer, too!

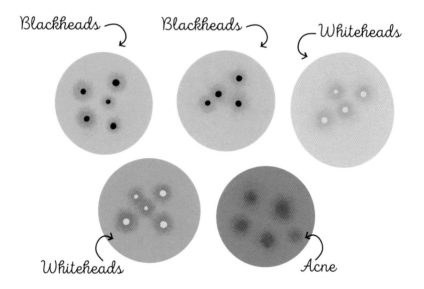

Blackheads

Blackheads

Whiteheads

Whiteheads

Acne

ANNOYING ACNE

I had acne as a teenager, which started when I was about fourteen. I tried lots of things, like washes and creams, to try and help my skin. But then when it still didn't get better, I went to visit the doctor for some treatment. After that, my skin got lots better! This lasted until I was about twenty-seven, then all of a sudden, my acne came back! Now I am thirty-two, and still have problems with acne. Part of my problem is that I am really bad at not picking my spots, which makes them worse and scars my skin!

Even as an adult, having acne has made me feel very self-conscious at times, always wondering if other people are noticing my spots. I just try and tell myself that everyone else is more interested in themselves and aren't looking at my skin! Or I try and focus on other things I like about myself, like my hair. I wanted to share this with you so that you know if you are worrying about acne, you aren't alone! It is so important to speak to someone if your skin is getting worse and it is bothering you. The earlier you get treatment, the fewer issues you will have with things like scarring. Acne is such a common problem – **it's not embarrassing at all** – and can be treated. Recently, I saw a doctor again and they are helping me try new treatments to make it better. So don't be ashamed – speak to a grown-up if your skin is troublesome!

Sadly, there's no sure way to prevent getting spots or acne. Almost every teenager has a few spots, and about one in five teenagers will have sufficient problems to need to see their doctor to get some help treating their skin. **However, there are some things you can do to try and reduce how often you break out and how serious your breakouts are:**

It's important to *wash your skin*, especially after exercise, to remove excess surface oils and dead skin cells that clog your pores. However, over-washing can actually damage your skin, by drying it out or irritating spots that are already there, so don't go scrubbing every five minutes!

If you use products on your skin, like creams, lotions or make-up, choose ones which won't block your pores, known as '*non-comedogenic*' or '*non-acnegenic*'.

If you can't live without hairspray or styling gel, try to keep it away from your face when you use it, as it's likely to include *sticky oils* that can make acne worse.

If you get acne on your chest or back, *avoid wearing tight clothes*, which can rub and cause irritation.

ASK DOCTOR EMILY

Q: *Should I pop my spots?*

A: The short answer is: no, you shouldn't. Popping them won't always get rid of them, and may clog up your pores even more! You might even end up causing an infection, or giving yourself a scar. Your spots will go away on their own, so by far the best option is to be patient, and wait for a pimple to disappear. If you really can't stop, and must pop, then there are a few things to bear in mind:

- **NEVER** pop a red, purple or brown spot without an obvious head. It will be very sore, and you'll do more damage than good.

- **ALWAYS** wash and dry your hands before touching your face.

- Rest a warm and clean flannel on your face for a few minutes, to help soften the skin around your spot, making it easier for it to just pop on its own.

- **For a whitehead**, use clean tweezers to gently poke the centre of the spot. It should pop and drain away. If it doesn't, it's probably not ready to pop, so leave it be! Don't use your fingernails in place of tweezers, as they could damage your skin and spread bacteria.

- **For a blackhead**, put cotton pads around your fingertips and press gently inward towards the spot. If the content doesn't come out, then stop squeezing. Again, the spot might just not be ready.

Part Two:

CHANGES IN YOUR MIND

Changing Brains

Over the last few chapters, you've discovered some of the changes that will happen to your body, but there are some major things happening in your mind, too! Your emotions, ways of thinking, and even parts of your personality are about to go on a wild ride, but once you've ridden the rollercoaster, things will settle down!

You probably feel much more grown up now than you did five years ago, and in five years' time, you're likely to feel different again. This doesn't mean you're going to transform into a completely new person, but your brain will go through a few changes over the coming years.

When we're very little, we think everything revolves around **US**. Our whole world is made up of our family and close friends. But as we get older, we start becoming more interested in the wider world. You might start to follow the news, and take an interest in people from different places or cultures. As teenagers, people often feel more connected and engaged with the world around them. Take someone like *Greta Thunberg* – as a teen, she became so passionate about fighting global warming and climate change that she started a worldwide movement! Not all of us can be as amazing as Greta, but she's a good example of a teen who opened her eyes to an important issue. Her story also shows what a huge difference young people like you can make if you set your mind to it!

Your brain is made up of lots of different sections, which all have important jobs to do. The earliest changes in your brain happen when you're about eleven years old. The front part of your brain – called the *frontal lobe* – starts to get more powerful. It's the part of the brain that controls your impulses and stops you from making rushed decisions, and it's done a lot of growing up already! If you know any toddlers, you'll notice that they are **NOT** very rational and rush into lots of impulsive decisions – for example, if there was someone holding a bag of their favourite sweets on the other side of a road, they would probably try to run over and grab the sweets without looking whether any cars were coming! As you get older, your frontal lobe develops; it's what helps you remember to slow down and look first, before you cross that road. You still want the sweets, but the sensible bit of your brain says they're not worth running in front of traffic for!

TAKING RISKS

However, that front part of your brain isn't fully developed until you're around thirty years old, and there's another part of your brain that develops during puberty which starts encouraging you to try new things. This is helpful in some ways – there are loads of new things you're going to want to try as you grow up, from learning to drive to living on your own or with friends. However, this part of your brain can sometimes be unhelpful, as trying risky activities without fully assessing the situation can be dangerous! For example, if you've never mountain biked before, but decide one day to try it out and go down the toughest, most advanced slope, there's a chance you'll end up hurt. Or if you decide to try smoking or drinking alcohol without stopping to think whether it's a sensible and safe idea first, you might run into trouble there, too. **Making a decision without thinking it through is not always a wise move.**

You'll probably make a few mistakes during your teenage years **– everybody does!** But learning from these mistakes is what helps us grow into independent and confident adults. By the time the *'sensible'* front part of our brain gets in full control, we've generally worked out our limits and can enjoy life as a grown-up in a safe and happy way.

First Crushes

As you grow up, you might start feeling attracted to other people in a more-than-friends way. It might take you a while to realize, but if you find yourself thinking about someone **ALL THE TIME,** imagining getting close to them or even kissing them, chances are you're feeling attracted to them. If both of you feel the same way, you may want to start a relationship. This may not sound like you now, but it is something that most people do feel like at some stage as they get older, for example as a teenager or an adult. Some people have their first close relationship as a teenager, and some people don't have their first relationship until they're in their twenties. There's no rush, and you shouldn't feel pressure to start having crushes on people or getting into a relationship until you feel ready.

UPS AND DOWNS

As you go through puberty, all the hormones in your body can play havoc with your emotions. Add to that all the changes going on in your brain and you might find yourself flipping between feeling fine one moment, and down in the dumps the next. There are all kinds of emotions your brain can feel, and it's a good idea to get to know them.

Next time you're feeling a bit rubbish, try to pinpoint exactly what emotion you're going through. **Do you feel...**

STRESSED?   LOW?   LONELY?

SAD?   TIRED?

WORRIED?   BORED?

And when you're feeling good, you could take a moment to think about that too. **Do you feel...**

PROUD?   PEACEFUL?   HAPPY

CREATIVE?   HOPEFUL?

CONTENTED?   CONFIDENT?

Understanding your emotions is the first step to being able to manage them. If we know that we're stressed, for example, we can recognize that we need to put aside some time to relax or do something fun, before returning to whatever task is stressing us out.

However, even if we understand them, sometimes emotions can still be tricky to manage. *Life is full of challenges*, and over the next few years you're likely to experience some tough ones, from exam pressure to falling out with friends. Sometimes, these **BIG** life things lead to **BIG** emotions that can get the best of us. If this is happening to you, the first thing you should do is tell somebody you trust, like a parent or other family member. Sometimes, it can be easier to talk to someone who is a bit more distant from the worries you are facing, like a teacher or counsellor. *Chatting through how you're feeling with someone might help you to see things a bit more clearly.*

As well as talking to somebody else, remember to talk to **YOURSELF** kindly. When we're feeling pants, it's easy for the little voice in our head to turn nasty, and tell us we're embarrassing or useless. Instead, try to remember that you are *amazing*, *unique* and *loved*. You can even say some positive words to yourself in front of your bathroom mirror – **saying things out loud helps your brain to believe them!**

"YOU DON'T NEED TO BE PERFECT – YOU'RE AMAZING JUST THE WAY YOU ARE!"

"AW, THANKS!"

ASK DOCTOR EMILY

Q: *I'm feeling down ALL the time. Is that normal?*

A: It's normal to experience ups and downs as you go through puberty, and you're likely to have some new and confusing emotions. However, if you're worried about the way you're feeling then it's important to ask for help. You might feel that you're not enjoying activities you used to like doing, or that you're worried or stressed all the time. If you're having difficulty getting to sleep, or concentrating, or you don't feel like eating, then these are things you should talk to someone about, too.

Our mental health – which means the healthiness of our minds – is really important. Everyone has times that are more stressful I or difficult during their teenage years. If you're struggling then it is nothing to be ashamed of, but it is something to address rather than ignore. It is not your fault that you are feeling the way you do, and you are not alone: lots of people struggle with their mental health at some point during their lives. Speak to someone in your family, a teacher or a doctor about what you are going through. There are also some phone numbers for mental health helplines at the back of this book, which you can call if you feel like you need to talk to somebody.

Body Confidence

In the 'Changing Shape' section, we talked about how girls' bodies change to be different shapes during puberty. **ALL BODIES ARE WONDERFUL**, whatever shape or size they are, but it's really easy to compare our bodies to someone else's and wish we looked like them. It's common to think about whether our bodies are normal or not, but for some people, this can turn into something they worry about a lot. They might get obsessed about a part of their body they wish they could change, or even look in the mirror and not see themselves for what they truly look like.

Having a healthy body image means accepting your body and the way you look. If you feel good about yourself, then you'll feel happier overall and get more out of life. This will also mean you have good self-esteem, which means you see yourself in a positive light, and as someone worthy of respect from others, which you are! Like we talked about earlier, by looking at yourself as a whole person, and not focusing on the little bits of yourself you might not like, you can boost your self-esteem. The way you look is only one small part of what makes you, you. Your brilliant personality, your achievements, your passions and your skills are all much more important.

ASK DOCTOR EMILY

Q: Why don't I look like the girls I see on social media?

A: It's important to remember that lots of the photos we see online or in magazines have been taken by professional photographers, or with flattering lighting, and edited to make the people look flawless. Spots, stretch marks, wrinkles or blemishes have been removed, and body parts might even have been tweaked to look bigger or smaller. So try to remember that when you wish you looked like someone you've seen online, they might not look quite like that in real life themselves! They're still beautiful, of course, but they have flaws like every other human. Try to stay focused on doing the things you enjoy, and keeping your body healthy, instead of worrying about the tiny details of what you look like.

The other thing to remember is that social media tends to only show one side of someone – their appearance – without showing all the other things that make them amazing humans, such as their sense of fun, their kindness, or their funniness. On social media, we can only view photos and videos, which don't often show these more important parts of a person, which you only get to know when you meet them.

STAY SAFE ONLINE

Please remember the golden rules of online life:

Think about waiting until you're 13 to use social media. Keep your location and personal information **private**.

Be smart – don't agree to meet face-to-face with an online friend, or send them photos of yourself, until you've spoken to an adult you trust.

Report anything abusive or that makes you feel uncomfortable to a trusted adult.

Remember your digital footprint – **everything you post online is permanent**.

Healthy Habits

A perfect body is one that works just the way it should, and not one that looks a certain way. To feel good about ourselves and keep everything in our bodies working properly, we all need to do regular exercise and eat well. It's important to have a good relationship with food, where we understand what things are good for us, and which are better to have as a more occasional treat. Our body needs a balance of different kinds of foods, so it can get all the nutrition it needs for all its different functions.

HERE ARE SOME TIPS FOR EATING HEALTHILY:

Eat lots of *fruits and vegetables*. They're packed with vitamins and minerals that keep your body healthy. You should aim for around five portions a day – a portion is about a handful.

Be aware of how much sugar you eat. *Sugar* isn't only in sweets and chocolate, but often hidden in food and drink that looks healthy, like fruit juices and breakfast cereals! Having too much sugar can cause problems like tooth decay, so it's best to save foods high in sugar for an occasional treat, rather than having them every day.

Drink lots of **water**. You need about six to eight cups of water a day to feel at your best, and even more if it's hot or you are exercising. Your body is made of about 60% water, so it needs regular top-ups to replace what you wee or sweat out!

Eat foods high in protein and **Omega-3**. Omega-3 are special types of fat which play an important role in keeping your body healthy. If you eat fish, salmon, tuna and cod are bursting with beneficial Omega-3. If you're vegetarian, eggs, nuts and seeds are an excellent source of protein and also contain Omega-3.

Watch out for **saturated fats**. We all need some fat in our diet to keep us healthy, but saturated fats aren't good for our bodies. They're in foods like cakes, biscuits and fatty meat, and you should try not to eat too much of them in your day-to-day life.

ASK DOCTOR EMILY

Q: I'm worried about how much I weigh. What should I do?

A: Lots of people worry about how much they weigh, and think it might be too high or too low. How much you weigh will depend on lots of things, including your height and your build. It's not a good idea to compare your weight to your friends', as they are likely to have different body shapes to you!

Food gives us energy, which is measured in calories. All food has calories in, and how many calories you eat affects how much you weigh. As you go about your day, you use up energy, meaning you use up calories, so it's all about finding a balance between what you put in your body and what your body uses up. When you exercise, your body needs lots of energy, so it uses up more calories. If you don't eat enough calories, your body uses up the fat it has stored and you become underweight. If you take in more calories than your body needs to use, then your body stores these calories as extra fat. Being very underweight or very overweight as an adult isn't good for you, and can even shorten your life, so it's a great idea to try and maintain a healthy weight.

If you do feel worried about your weight, the first thing to do is chat to your parents about it. They might suggest visiting your doctor, who can reassure you that you're healthy, or talk to you about things that could help you lose weight, or put it on, depending on what would be best for you and your body.

SUPER SLEEP

Because your body and mind are growing so quickly during puberty, they need lots of energy. To have lots of energy, you need to get plenty of sleep. If you want to feel your best, you should aim to get about **eight to ten hours of sleep a night**. If you're having trouble concentrating, or it's difficult to get up in the morning, or you need a nap as soon as get home from school, you're probably not getting enough sleep at night.

Keeping Active

One of the best things you can do for your body is to stay active! When we exercise, we build muscle, strengthen our hearts and improve our blood circulation. Exercise is also good for our minds, as it helps relieve stress and anxiety and boosts self-esteem. It also produces 'feel good' hormones called endorphins, which make us feel happy and calm. And exercise doesn't have to be boring! You might be someone who loves jumping jacks or push-ups, but if you're not, there are lots of other things you could try…

WALKING   DANCING

CYCLING

RUNNING   ROLLERBLADING

HOCKEY   ICE SKATING

FOOTBALL   NETBALL

PLAYING IN THE PARK

RUGBY   JUDO

Team sports are especially good, as not only are you exercising, but you're developing social skills, too. By taking part in a group activity, you're likely to make friendships and build bonds with your teammates. And it's not all about the highs! Going through lows in team sports can help you build resilience, which is such an important superpower to have in life. *Resilience* is the ability to face problems and hard times head on, and bounce back from them. When playing a sport, you might build resilience by getting through a gruelling game or accepting a tough defeat. The skills you gain on the pitch or court can then be transferred to other situations in life, and they might even help you get through a stressful time. Say you fail a test at school or fall out with your friends, you'll have built enough resilience to quickly recover from the situation and **come back stronger!**

DRUGS, DRINKING AND SMOKING

As you grow up and become more independent, you'll be faced with lots of choices. Sometimes, these choices are going to be tough, and the decisions you make can have an impact on your life for years to come. For example, you might have friends that start drinking alcohol, smoking cigarettes or taking drugs. You may feel pressure to try them too, even if it's not really what you want to do.

In the UK, if you are under eighteen years old, it is **illegal** for you to buy alcohol or have alcohol bought for you. It is **illegal** to take drugs at any age. This means that if you get caught doing these things, you could be **arrested**, **fined money** or get a **criminal record**, which might make it harder for you to get a job or travel abroad when you are older. In addition to being illegal, drugs and alcohol are **harmful to your body**. Some drugs can be very dangerous. They can make you incredibly ill if you take too much of them, and even put you at risk of dying. Many are also **addictive**, meaning that if you try them a few times, you may find you crave them again and again, making it difficult to stop taking them. Alcohol can also make you very unwell if you have too much of it, and can change your behaviour so you're more likely to take dangerous risks. It's best to wait until you are legally old enough to try alcohol, then have a small amount at a time to avoid feeling out of control, or being ill the next day.

These days, there's a much better understanding of the dangers of smoking than there was fifty years ago, when lots of young people used to do it. Like drugs and alcohol, smoking cigarettes damages your body, filling your lungs with harmful substances and putting pressure on your heart, too. You might have heard that e-cigarettes or vaping isn't as bad for you as smoking, and while that might be true, inhaling any chemicals (in this case, *nicotine*) into your lungs is not likely to be good for you! Vaping can also be addictive, and sometimes leads people on to smoking cigarettes. It's also such a new thing that more studies need to be done to make sure the chemicals aren't doing damage that we're not aware of yet. **With that in mind, it's best to just steer clear!**

Be True to Yourself

As we grow up, we get to know ourselves better than we ever have before. Trying new activities, exploring new ideas and making new friends helps us to work out the kind of people we want to be as adults. This book has focused on the physical and mental changes in female bodies and minds. But what does it mean to be female? Female and male are words used to describe somebody's sex – basically which body parts you are born with. If you are born with female body parts, doctors put 'female' on your birth certificate. But there's another word we use to talk about being male or female, and that is 'gender'. This is slightly different because, while the term 'sex' refers to our bodies, 'gender identity' can refer to how we feel about ourselves, regardless of what body parts we have.

As we discussed earlier in the book, our identities are made up of so much more than what our bodies looks like, so even if you think you know someone's sex or gender from the way they look, you may not be right. It's really important to **respect** everyone's feelings about who they are. Some people might be born with male body parts, but feel deeply that inside their heart and mind they are female, or vice versa. It can take many years for someone to be sure that their gender identity isn't the same as the sex they were born with. If you feel confused about your identity, then it's important to chat it through with a parent or doctor. In time, things that are really unclear as you're growing up can fall into place and become just *part of you*, so never hurry yourself to fit into any particular label or group until you really know what you want that label to be.

SMASHING STEREOTYPES

Whatever being a *girl* means to you, it shouldn't ever include looking or acting a certain way. In the past, girls and women had lots of limits put on them. They weren't expected to have jobs, but to stay at home and look after a husband and children. People didn't think they should go to university, or vote in elections. **Luckily, times have changed, and most girls and women can now do what they want and be whoever they want to be.** Some women choose to have children, and some people choose not to. I have an amazing job as a doctor, as well as a lovely family! Years ago, there were no female doctors, only males. When I was at university, there were actually more girls than boys in my year group. It just goes to show how things have changed over the years. *The most important thing is that you work hard to achieve your goals, whatever they are!*

DIFFERENT IS GOOD

As you go through life, you'll meet people from lots of different cultures, backgrounds and religions, of all different physical abilities and ages. Another word for the differences between people is *diversity*. Diversity is something to be celebrated – if everyone looked and acted exactly the same, the world would be a very dull place! It's important to respect someone wherever they come from, whatever they look like and whatever they believe in. **We can all learn a lot from each other!** Choose to be accepting and understanding of people's different beliefs and abilities, and you'll be helping to make the world a kinder place.

Families, Friends and Feeling Supported

When lots of things are changing, it's good to have people around us we can turn to for support and guidance; people who will be there for us, no matter what. As you go through puberty, your relationships with your friends and family may go through some changes. When you're little, you rely on your family to look after you, to make you food and even tidy up your things. As you grow up, you'll start to take on some of these responsibilities yourself and may find you want more independence than your family is giving you! But it's important to remember that everyone still needs help sometimes, so try not to push your family away and don't feel bad about admitting you need support.

DIFFERENT KINDS OF FAMILIES

There are all kinds of different family set-ups, and your family may look a bit different from some of your friends' families.

Some people live with both their mum and their dad. They might be the only child in the family, or have lots of brothers or sisters, like I did **(FOUR brothers – argh!)**.

Some people live in a single-parent family. If their parents have separated, then they may live with just one of them. Sometimes, they might split their time between both parents, and live in two different homes. Some people live with step-parents. If one or both of their parents have chosen to be with a new partner, they might call them their stepmum or stepdad. If their step-parents have children from previous relationships, then they are usually called stepsisters or stepbrothers. Some people may live with two mums or two dads, in a same-sex parent family – *families come in all sorts of shapes and sizes!*

Some people live in adopted families. You may have heard the term *'adoption'* and wondered what it meant. This means the parents who gave birth to a child (*the birth family*) were not able to look after them during their childhood. This can be for lots of complicated reasons. Another set of parents (*called the adoptive parents*) welcome the child into their own family, where they love and support them.

Some people live with foster parents. A *foster family* provides a safe and caring home for a child when birth parents are not able to look after their children. There can be lots of different reasons why this is. Sometimes children are in foster care for a short period of time while temporary problems are sorted out, sometimes it can be for much longer periods of time.

In addition to your family members, there are lots of other people in your community who might be in your support network. Some children have social workers, whose job it is to look out for them and their family. School nurses and local GPs are also good people to bring into your support network if you're worried about your health. *Whatever your support network looks like, there's no normal!* And remember, **YOU** might be part of someone's support network, too, so look out for your friends and family members and be kind! ♥

Part Three:

WHAT ABOUT THE BOYS?

We're nearly at the end of the book, but there's just enough time to have a quick chat about what **BOYS GO THROUGH** during puberty. Puberty usually starts a year or two later for boys than it does for girls. Just like for us, their brain conducts all the changes using hormones, but different hormones come into play. While a lot of the changes in girls' bodies are due to the hormone oestrogen, in boys' bodies it is the hormone testosterone which has the starring role.

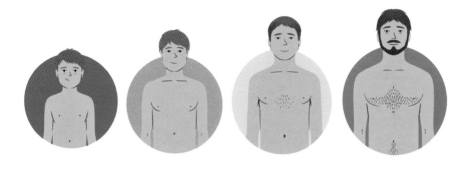

Testosterone triggers hair to grow on boys' faces. They might grow a moustache under their nose and a beard over the bottom half of their face and their chin, but this takes a long time and doesn't usually develop until their later teenage years or even their twenties. Boys often start to shave at around fourteen to sixteen years old but don't get full facial hair until much later.

Testosterone causes boys' voice boxes to grow, **which makes their voices deeper.** Because this takes a bit of time to settle down, their voice might get a bit squeaky every now and then. Boys can feel embarrassed or self-conscious about this, so try to be kind and not tease them.

Boys' **skin gets oilier** and they might get spots or acne.

Testosterone also **makes hair grow** on boys' bodies, including on their arms, legs, under their armpits and around their genital area. They might get hair on their chest, too. Boys' body hair usually ends up being a bit darker and thicker than girls'.

Like girls, boys go through **growth spurts**. As they get taller, they may look a bit gangly for a few years. Later in puberty, their muscles will grow so they'll start to look a bit bulkier.

Boys' **body shape changes** as their shoulders and chest get broader.

Like girls, **boys get sweatier** during puberty, so often need to start using an antiperspirant.

Boys' bodies can't make babies, so they **don't have periods**.

Boys' **penises and testicles gets bigger**. Their testicles start making sperm.

A TRICKY TIME

The idea of puberty can make boys just as nervous as it can make girls. Even though they're not going through all the same changes as you, what they go through can be awkward and nerve-wracking as well. Like you, their thoughts and feelings will be affected by the hormones in their body, so they can go through lots of ups and downs. Sometimes, boys feel pressure to keep their feelings bottled up and act 'manly', so they might not let on just how low they're feeling. Let your male friends know it's **OK** to share their feelings, and try to be patient and understanding with them.

In the same way you'd be annoyed or upset if someone made fun of the changes you are going through, don't poke fun at the changes boys are going through either.

So what now?

AN AMAZING JOURNEY

And that's it – that's all you need to know about growing up!
Well, maybe not quite. Because, really, to learn everything
there is to know about growing up, you have to go through it.
You have to go over those highs, down those lows and travel
around those twists and turns. But now that you've read this
book, hopefully you're feeling ready for the amazing journey
that is to come.

You've learned about the changes that will happen to your body, from developing breasts, to growing hair, to starting your period. You've discovered some of the thoughts and feelings you might experience as you go through puberty, and why these might happen. And you've also been given some tips for looking after yourself. That's a lot of information to take in! But the good thing about books is that you can read them **again and again**. So, you can always flick back and check a chapter if you've forgotten some of the information in it.

I hope you're feeling confident and excited about your future. I remember when I was getting ready to go to secondary school, thinking how many changes I would go through in the next few years. At the start of the journey, it can feel like such a long road! But as soon as you begin, it just flies by. I ended up being a really late starter with puberty, so was nearly finishing secondary school before anything happened! So, you just never know how it will be for you. **The most important thing is that you try and have as much fun as possible!** Although teenage years can be tricky, they are also an incredible time where you learn all about the person you will become.

If you still have concerns or questions, there are lots of places to go to for advice, and you can find links to some of these at the back of the book. Grown-ups are a good source of knowledge too, as they've already been through all this puberty stuff, so don't feel embarrassed about talking to your parents or a doctor if you're still feeling curious.

So, put your best foot forward and take a deep breath. It's your journey, and you're going to do it your way.

Watch out, world – amazing, unique, confident **YOU** *is coming through.*

GLOSSARY

Acne A skin condition which causes spots and oily skin.

Body odour A smell made by bacteria breaking down sweat.

Breasts (boobs) The soft parts on the front of women's and older girls' chests. Women have breasts so they can make milk to feed their babies. (Not all women choose to do this though!)

Cervix The opening at the bottom of the uterus.

Discharge Whiteish fluid which cleans and moisturizes the vagina.

Emotions Feelings, such as happiness, sadness or anger.

Genitals The parts of men and women's bodies which are involved in making babies. Girls' genitals are mostly on the inside of their bodies and include the uterus (womb), ovaries and vagina. Boys' genitals are mainly on the outside of their bodies and include the testicles and penis.

Hormones Chemicals in the body that act like messengers, telling your body what to do and when. Different hormones do different things: some control the way you digest food, some control how and when you grow, and some get your body ready to become an adult.

Labia Folds of skin which cover a woman's vagina.

Ligament A short band of tough tissue that connects bones or supports muscles.

Oestrogen A hormone which plays various roles in the body, including making breast tissue grow.

Ovaries The organs in female bodies which produce egg cells.

Penis The part of male bodies through which sperm and urine are released.

Period When a bit of blood is lost from the vagina each month. Periods start during puberty.

Pituitary gland A little gland in the centre of the brain that organizes the hormones and messages the body needs to go through puberty. Some people think of it like the 'conductor of the orchestra' because it makes everything happen at the right time and in the right order.

Puberty The physical process of your body and mind growing into an adult's.

Pubic hair Hair that grows near your genital area.

Sperm Special cells made inside male bodies which, if they meet with an egg in a female body, can grow into a baby.

Testicles (balls) The organs in which sperm cells are made in male bodies.

Uterus (womb) The organ in female bodies where babies grow during pregnancy. It stretches to get bigger as a baby inside it gets bigger.

Vagina A tube inside female bodies that connects the uterus (womb) to the outside of the body.

USEFUL LINKS

You can find out more about puberty and growing up through the following links. There are also some websites you can visit, or numbers you can call, if you are going through a difficult time and need someone to talk to.

Periods

CBBC www.bbc.co.uk/newsround/56267456

NHS www.nhs.uk/conditions/periods/

Spots and Acne

KidsHealth www.kidshealth.org/en/teens/prevent-acne.html

NHS www.nhs.uk/conditions/acne/

Personal Hygiene and Keeping Clean

KidsHealth www.kidshealth.org/en/teens/hygiene-basics.html.

Body Image

CBBC www.bbc.co.uk/cbbc/findoutmore/help-me-out-body-image

Healthy Living

British Heart Foundation www.bhf.org.uk/informationsupport/support/healthy-living

NHS www.nhs.uk/change4life

Mental Health and Emotional Support

Young Minds (Support for children and young people struggling with their mental health) www.youngminds.org.uk

Beat (Support for children and young people suffering with eating disorders) www.beateatingdisorders.co.uk

CALM (Listening services and support for anyone who needs to talk) Helpline: 0800 58 58 58
www.thecalmzone.net

Childline (Support for children and young people in the UK)
Helpline: 0800 1111
www.childline.org.uk

FRANK (Confidential advice and information about drugs, their effects and the law) Helpline: 0300 123 6600
www.talktofrank.com

Happy Maps (A great resource for each age group discussing mental health issues)
www.happymaps.co.uk

INDEX